Thank You Mama

A Book Of Gratitude for New Moms

Written by Meridith Lasko
Illustrated by Teddy Biron

Copyright © 2024 Meridith Lasko
All rights reserved.

This is a work of fiction. Names, characters, places, and incidents are either a product of the author's imagination or are used fictitiously, and any resemblance to actual persons, living or dead, business establishments, events, or locales is entirely coincidental. No part of this book may be reproduced or transmitted in any form or by any means, graphic, electronic, or mechanical, including photocopying recording, or taping without the written consent of the author or publisher.

Briley & Baxter Publications | Plymouth, Massachusetts

ISBN: 978-1-961978-31-7

Book Design: Stacy Padula

This book is dedicated to *Marina* and *Laurel*. Thank you for opening a whole new world to me. Being a mom is the greatest gift in the world. If you become moms someday, I hope I can be just as supportive to you as my parents are to me.

_____   __/__/__

To:

From:

♥ _____

You are doing an amazing job, *Mama*.

Thank you for taking such good care of
me all day and all night.

I know you must be tired, hungry, and lonely, but you make sure I am rested, fed, and loved.

I am so lucky to be your baby. Since the moment we met, I have known I would *love you* forever.

I know some moments are amazing, while others are hard, but you are doing a great job at making me feel safe, secure, and loved. *I am so proud of you!*

Every day, you will get better and better at being a mother.
I will always see you as *perfect!*
I can't wait to grow and become a toddler…

…but right now I am so little and need you so much.
We are both learning together,
and I think we are doing a *great* job!

Please remember to be patient and kind to yourself.
You are *amazing*.

I love you so much. Thank you, *Mama.*

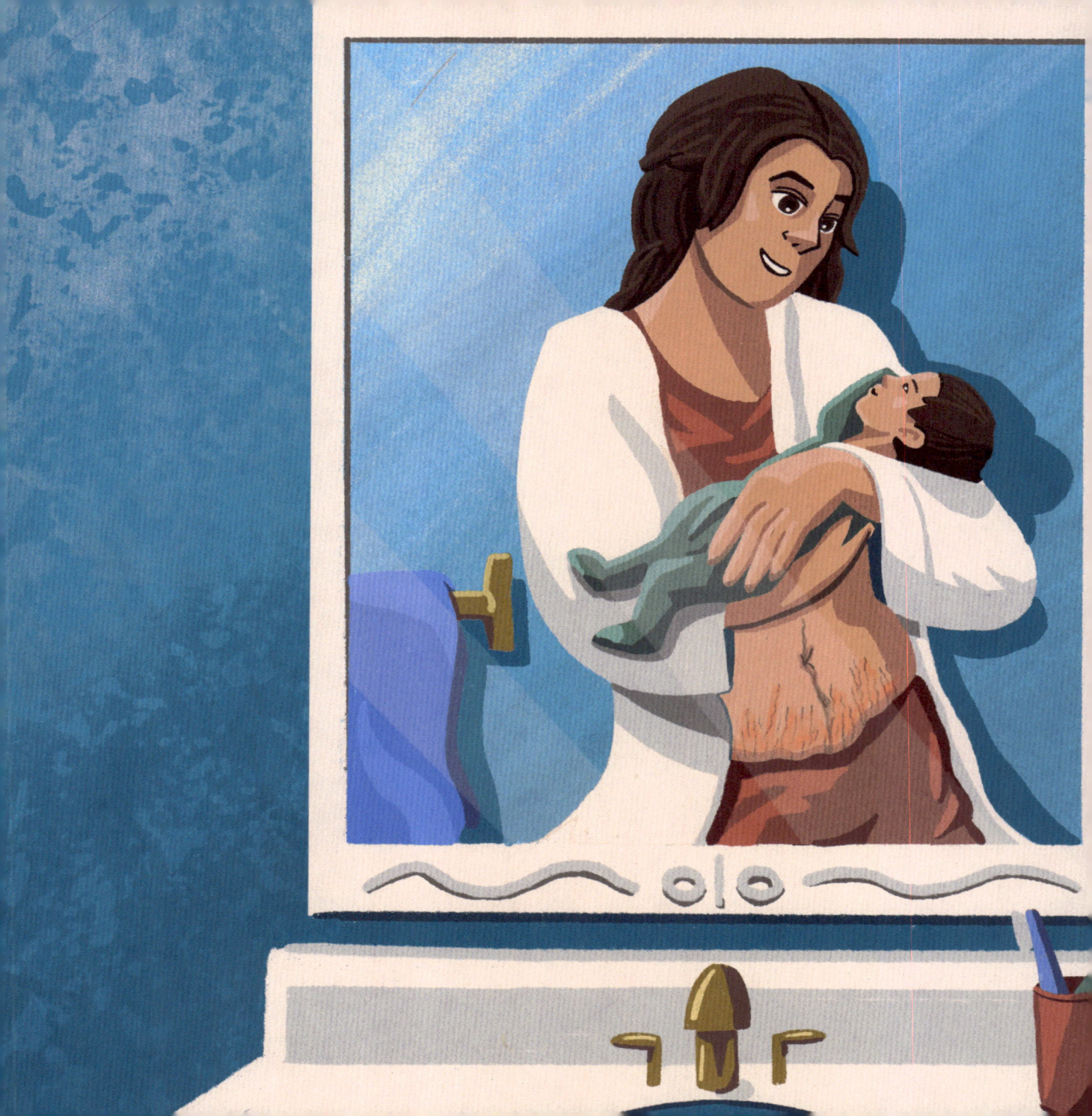

About the Author

Meridith Lasko lives on Cape Cod with her husband and two young daughters. She enjoys taking advantage of all the beautiful nature and enriching community opportunities in her day-to-day life. Originally from New Hampshire, she settled on Cape Cod to raise her family.

Meridith wrote this book after the birth of her second daughter. "Moms read a lot of books to their babies, and the content is normally directed towards the baby. I wanted to write something for the new mom. Becoming a mom is challenging, no matter what your circumstances are. This book is a way to encourage moms everywhere and bring a bit of positivity to them. You can never have enough. Every mom should be given this book and all the support they can get." – Meridith

About the Illustrator

Teddy Biron is a young artist and author from Cape Cod. He graduated Sandwich High School in 2020. He likes to work with vivid colors and loose concepts. Painting in watercolor and acrylic has been a passion of his as well. His book "The Lighthouse Keeper Saves the Bay" is an Amazon bestseller. He has won several awards including: Third place in the painting category of the Congressional Art Competition First place in the Cape Cod Art Centers Beginnings Exhibit as well as first Place through the Sandwich Art Alliance. He debuted in the Reverdy Galleries small works show in 2019 , and his own show in December of 2019 and January of 2020.

www.ingramcontent.com/pod-product-compliance
Lightning Source LLC
Chambersburg PA
CBHW042054050526
44107CB00110B/1147